100 QUESTIONS
~ FOR ~
DAD

A JOURNAL TO INSPIRE
REFLECTION AND CONNECTION

JEFF BOGLE

ROCKRIDGE PRESS

For general information on our other products and services or to obtain technical support, please contact our Customer Care Department within the U.S. at (866) 744-2665, or outside the U.S. at (510) 253-0500.

Rockridge Press publishes its books in a variety of electronic and print formats. Some content that appears in print may not be available in electronic books, and vice versa.

TRADEMARKS: Rockridge Press and the Rockridge Press logo are trademarks or registered trademarks of Callisto Media Inc. and/or its affiliates, in the United States and other countries, and may not be used without written permission. All other trademarks are the property of their respective owners. Rockridge Press is not associated with any product or vendor mentioned in this book.

Interior and Cover Designer: Regina Stadnik
Art Producer: Tom Hood
Editor: Carolyn Abate
Production Editor: Matthew Burnett
Production Manager: Martin Worthington

Cover and interior illustrations courtesy of Shutterstock. Author photograph courtesy of Bryan Sargent Photography.

Paperback ISBN: 978-1-63807-956-9
R0

THIS BOOK BELONGS TO:

_____

CONTENTS

INTRODUCTION

My dad would often talk about playing basketball on the streets of West Philadelphia and tell stories of his time in the Army. I remember hearing about his "famous" left hook shot on the basketball court. He used to go on about the frigid training exercises he endured in Alaska, as well as skiing and snowshoeing. It was hard to imagine the dad I knew ever doing any of those things! When I was a little kid, he told me about the time he went to the Seattle World's Fair in 1962, and decades later, while bouncing me on his lap, he still mourned the souvenirs left behind in a taxicab.

I never thought to ask him for more details as he told his stories. For example, how did my 5'9" father compete against the taller kids on the court? Is that why he learned the hook shot? Did it take him long to learn how to snowshoe? How did it feel being up high in the newly built Space Needle? And what exactly did he leave in that taxi?

When I lost my dad in the summer of 2020, I also lost his stories, and suddenly realized that there's so much about him I never knew and now, unfortunately, never will. I wish my dad had been gifted a guided journal like this, a journal with a series of prompts to jog his memory and unearth long-forgotten anecdotes. It would have given him the chance to immortalize his 82 years of life.

I've created this journal so that you can preserve your story—for yourself and for those who adore you. You'll tell your story in your own voice and share it with the people you love most. Once completed, this book will serve as a meaningful keepsake, a window into who you were and are, what and who you love, and all that you've learned along the way.

As you respond to each prompt, try to be as candid as possible and allow yourself the opportunity to be vulnerable. Let your true self pour out onto these pages and know how impactful it will be for loved ones to have and hold on to this story, your story, told through your one-of-a-kind perspective.

Each question is designed to encourage you to write freely about your origin story, what early family life was like, your passions, and personal fatherhood journey—and to share the dreams you have for the future. Finally, you'll impart some of the wisdom you've accumulated during a life well-lived.

Choose a comfy seat, find a great pen and use it throughout for continuity, and dig in. Feel free to bounce around between sections but don't overthink it. Have fun, let your emotions guide you, and soon you'll have transformed your incredible personal narrative into a tangible document that will be a treasured keepsake for decades to come.

PART I

THE EARLY YEARS

Every superhero has an origin story. The same is true of dads! Where you came from and how you grew up formed the foundation of the person and dad you are today. In this section, you'll tackle questions about your earliest years and memories and be asked to describe what family life was like when you were a child. Additionally, you'll have the chance to share your thoughts on school, friendships, and the traditions your family celebrated. The stories you tell here will give your loved ones a glimpse of a version of you they never knew.

ORIGIN STORY

What's your full name, and who named you? What is the significance or meaning of your name? Did you like your name growing up or use a nickname?

_____

_____

_____

_____

_____

_____

_____

_____

_____

When I was **YOUNG**, my **AMBITION** was to be one of the people who **MADE** a **DIFFERENCE** in this world. My **HOPE** is to leave the world a **LITTLE BETTER** for having been there.

JIM HENSON

When and where were you born? How was the story of that day told to you as you were growing up?

_____

_____

_____

_____

_____

_____

_____

_____

_____

_____

How would your parent(s) describe you as a baby and as a toddler? For example: were you fussy, loud, or giggly?

_____

_____

_____

_____

_____

_____

_____

_____

_____

Describe your earliest childhood memory that used any or all five senses—sight, smell, taste, sound, and touch. What feelings come with this memory?

_____

_____

_____

_____

_____

_____

_____

_____

What was the biggest challenge you overcame as a child?

_____

_____

_____

_____

_____

_____

_____

_____

_____

_____

_____

FAMILY

What was your dad like? What memories, positive or negative, do you have from your life together? If you didn't know him, describe how that felt while you were growing up.

_____

_____

_____

_____

_____

_____

_____

_____

All great **CHANGE** in America **BEGINS** at the dinner table.

RONALD REAGAN

What set your family apart from others in your neighborhood? Did your extended family—cousins, aunts and uncles, grandparents—live nearby or far away?

_____

_____

_____

_____

_____

_____

_____

_____

_____

Describe the home you grew up in. Was it an apartment or a house? Describe your favorite room in that home.

_____

_____

_____

_____

_____

_____

_____

_____

_____

What was dinnertime like in your family? What do you remember about being in the kitchen? Did you help cook and bake or get chased out?

_____

_____

_____

_____

_____

_____

_____

_____

What family stories were told to you while you were growing up? Share one that has stayed with you.

_____

_____

_____

_____

_____

_____

_____

_____

_____

_____

TRADITIONS

Describe your favorite family tradition. Did you carry it forward?
Do you still participate in this tradition today?

_____

_____

_____

_____

_____

_____

_____

_____

_____

"MY FATHER used to play with **MY BROTHER** and me in the yard. **MOTHER** would come out and say, 'You're tearing up the grass.' 'We're not raising grass,' **DAD** would reply. 'We're **RAISING BOYS.'"**

HARMON KILLEBREW

Which toys did you play with the most as a child? What was your favorite? What was its name? How did you play with this toy—did it act as your friend, did it come everywhere with you? Do you still have it or wish you did?

_____

_____

_____

_____

_____

_____

_____

_____

How did you experience the great outdoors? Did you have a backyard, ride your bike around the neighborhood, or spend time at a local park? What was your favorite part about being outside?

_____

_____

_____

_____

_____

_____

_____

_____

What was your favorite holiday growing up? How did you and your family celebrate it? How about birthdays? Describe your favorite birthday.

_____

_____

_____

_____

_____

_____

_____

_____

_____

What's an experience of your childhood that subsequent generations have missed out on? How did having this experience impact you when you were growing up?

_____

_____

_____

_____

_____

_____

_____

_____

_____

SCHOOL

What was your favorite subject in school as a child? What did you like about it? Which class was a struggle for you?

_____

_____

_____

_____

_____

_____

_____

_____

_____

I BELIEVE that what **WE BECOME** depends on what **OUR FATHERS** teach us at odd moments, when they aren't trying to **TEACH US**. We are formed by little scraps of **WISDOM**.

UMBERTO ECO

Were you concerned about getting good grades or was socializing your priority? If you asked your teachers and fellow students about yourself back then, what do you think they'd say?

_____

_____

_____

_____

_____

_____

_____

_____

Who were your best friends growing up? What kind of games and activities did you play and do together? Who do you still keep in touch with?

_____

_____

_____

_____

_____

_____

_____

Describe your after-school routine: Did you watch TV or get started right away on homework? What was your go-to after-school snack, and who prepared it for you?

_____

_____

_____

_____

_____

_____

_____

_____

What activities did you participate in during school? Which was your favorite, and which were you forced to do? Do you have regrets about not sticking with any of them longer?

_____

_____

_____

_____

_____

_____

_____

_____

PART II

PASSIONS AND PURSUITS

A unique blend of passions, values, and experiences have combined to make you a one-of-a-kind human being and a distinctive dad! This section is about adding vibrant details to your life story. You'll be asked about your favorite things, heroes who have paved the way for you, as well as the work you've accomplished and still wish to do. You'll touch on the beliefs you hold dear, and the places that continue to stir your emotions. Your answers to these questions will paint a fuller picture of what makes you who you are.

A FEW FAVORITES

Describe the best days of your childhood, the days you would want to go back in time to relive again and again.

_____

_____

_____

_____

_____

_____

_____

_____

"You gotta be really **DELIBERATE** with how you **CHOOSE** to spend your day because those are the **MOMENTS** you're away from **YOUR CHILD.**"

MAHERSHALA ALI

What was the finest gift you gave to someone? Who was the recipient and why was the gift so special? Describe the greatest gift you have received and who gave it to you.

_____

_____

_____

_____

_____

_____

_____

_____

What was your favorite book as a child? What memories do you have about reading it? What is your all-time favorite book and why?

_____

_____

_____

_____

_____

_____

_____

_____

_____

What did you enjoy doing most as a young adult? Do you still enjoy those same things?

_____

_____

_____

_____

_____

_____

_____

_____

_____

Who are your four favorite people, past or present, that you would like to invite to dinner? What's one question you would ask each guest?

_____

_____

_____

_____

_____

_____

_____

_____

JOBS AND OTHER INTERESTS

What did you want to be when you grew up? What steps did you take to try to attain that goal? What did you learn along the way?

_____

_____

_____

_____

_____

_____

_____

_____

> If I can **CREATE** the minimum of my **PLANS** and **DESIRES** there shall be **NO REGRETS.**

BESSIE COLEMAN

Describe the first job where you earned a paycheck. What was the best job you ever had? What were your roles and responsibilities at each?

_____

_____

_____

_____

_____

_____

_____

_____

Who and/or what do you credit with the success you've achieved throughout your working life?

_____

_____

_____

_____

_____

_____

_____

_____

_____

_____

Was your job demanding? How did you balance work life and family life? Do you feel you had enough time to be an actively engaged dad?

_____

_____

_____

_____

_____

_____

_____

_____

If you could switch careers right now, what would you love to do for a living and why?

_____

_____

_____

_____

_____

_____

_____

_____

_____

VALUES AND BELIEFS

What is the best piece of life advice you've received, and who gave it to you?

_____

_____

_____

_____

_____

_____

_____

_____

_____

The **TRUE TEST** of a man's **CHARACTER** is what he does when no one is **WATCHING**.

JOHN WOODEN

Name three core values that have guided your decision-making the most throughout life. Were those values taught to you, or did you develop them on your own?

_____

_____

_____

_____

_____

_____

_____

_____

_____

_____

Describe a situation you encountered where one of your beliefs was tested. How did you handle it? With hindsight, what would you have done differently?

_____

_____

_____

_____

_____

_____

_____

_____

If you suddenly came into a life-changing amount of money, what are the first few things you would choose to do with it?

_____

_____

_____

_____

_____

_____

_____

_____

_____

Name a dad you know whom you admire today. What makes them stand out, and have you two spoken about their approach to parenting and life?

_____

_____

_____

_____

_____

_____

_____

_____

MEMORABLE PLACES AND THINGS

Where are you most happy? For example, standing over a pan of sizzling onions in the kitchen? Sitting in your favorite team's home stadium? Or on an airplane flying someplace new? What is it about being in this moment that fills you with joy?

_____

_____

_____

_____

_____

_____

_____

"

There's no way I would have thought **FATHERHOOD** would've been the **ENTRYWAY** to realizing a lot of **MY DREAMS.**

"

LA GUARDIA CROSS

What was the most memorable event you have witnessed in person—a concert, sporting event, or political protest? What made it special?

_____

_____

_____

_____

_____

_____

_____

_____

What do you remember about the first time you experienced work by the artist (a musician, painter, actor, or author) who would go on to become your all-time favorite? Where were you and what were you doing when this art came into your life?

_____

_____

_____

_____

_____

_____

_____

_____

_____

What from your past are you nostalgic for today—maybe a vacation destination, TV show, an old hobby, or a way of life?

_____

_____

_____

_____

_____

_____

_____

_____

What is the greatest meal you ever ate? Where were you, who else was at the table, and what made it so memorable?

_____

_____

_____

_____

_____

_____

_____

_____

PART III

LOVE
AND
FRIENDSHIP

Throughout the course of a life, people you meet, spend time with and support, as well as those you choose to love, leave indelible marks. The questions in this section focus on your most special relationships. You will start with your very first experiences, both with friends and in romance. After that you'll move on to sharing stories of the most meaningful moments you have witnessed and words of wisdom you will never forget.

BIG FIRSTS

How old were you when you first kissed someone romantically?
Were you nervous? Was it planned or spontaneous? Who was
the recipient of that momentous smooch?

_____

_____

_____

_____

_____

_____

_____

_____

"MY FATHER gave me the **GREATEST GIFT** anyone could give another person: **HE BELIEVED IN ME."**

JIM VALVANO

What was your most memorable first date? Who was it with? Where did you go and what did the two of you do?

_____

_____

_____

_____

_____

_____

_____

_____

_____

Describe the first time you experienced the pang of a breaking heart. How did you bounce back, and what lessons did you learn?

_____

_____

_____

_____

_____

_____

_____

_____

_____

Describe a time when you made a good first impression on someone. What about when you didn't? If you could redo that experience, what would you do differently?

_____

_____

_____

_____

_____

_____

_____

_____

Who was your first close friend of a different gender? How old were each of you, and what made the friendship work?

_____

_____

_____

_____

_____

_____

_____

_____

_____

FRIENDS

What did friendship mean to you as a child? How has that definition evolved as you became an adult?

_____

_____

_____

_____

_____

_____

_____

_____

_____

She did not stand alone, but what stood behind her, the **MOST POTENT MORAL FORCE** in her life, was the **LOVE OF HER FATHER.**

HARPER LEE

Who is the person you've been friends with the longest? Why do you think you're still friends after all these years?

_____

_____

_____

_____

_____

_____

_____

_____

_____

What outlandish ideas did you and your childhood friends dream up? How did your adventures or inventions turn out?

_____

_____

_____

_____

_____

_____

_____

_____

Describe an experience when you needed to rely on a friend. Who was that person, and how did they help you get through the situation?

_____

_____

_____

_____

_____

_____

_____

_____

When were you a great friend to someone? Describe the moment that required you to support someone close to you.

_____

_____

_____

_____

_____

_____

_____

_____

_____

ROMANCE

What do you believe are the key elements to having a long, healthy, and happy romantic relationship?

_____

_____

_____

_____

_____

_____

_____

_____

_____

" First **BEST** is **FALLING IN LOVE**. Second best is **BEING IN LOVE**. Least best is falling out of love. But any of it is better than never having been in love. "

MAYA ANGELOU

Describe a lesson about love you learned the hard way. How did it feel to go through that experience?

_____

_____

_____

_____

_____

_____

_____

_____

_____

_____

What is the best decision you ever made concerning love? For example, maybe you worked extra hard to preserve an important relationship or you ended a less-than-healthy relationship.

_____

_____

_____

_____

_____

_____

_____

_____

_____

How do you demonstrate love? Do you show it through physical touch, positive words, giving gifts, or spending time with someone?

_____

_____

_____

_____

_____

_____

_____

_____

Where did your ideals about love come from? Was it family members, movies, or books? What relationships did you admire? How did they show you what it means to love?

_____

_____

_____

_____

_____

_____

_____

_____

INSPIRATIONS

What inspirational quote or motivational thought inspires you to this day? How has it impacted the way you live your life?

_____

_____

_____

_____

_____

_____

_____

_____

_____

MY FATHER didn't tell me how to live; he **LIVED AND LET ME WATCH HIM DO IT.**

CLARENCE BUDINGTON KELLAND

Aside from a family member, who was your hero growing up? What was it about this person that you admired, respected, or wanted to emulate?

_____

_____

_____

_____

_____

_____

_____

_____

Be it through words or actions, how do you think you've inspired others throughout your life?

_____

_____

_____

_____

_____

_____

_____

_____

_____

Now think about a time you observed unbecoming behavior.
How did it teach you what *not* to do?

_____

_____

_____

_____

_____

_____

_____

_____

_____

What's an experience you have had that changed your perception of yourself, and how so?

_____

_____

_____

_____

_____

_____

_____

_____

_____

PART IV

ON BEING A DAD

A dad's journey into and through fatherhood
is extraordinary. And yet, children are not always
gifted the opportunity to discover what has made their
dad special. Sure, they may know the hits but have never
heard the B-sides (some of them may need you to explain what
that means). The questions in this section will focus on your
child's or children's early years, your personal story of
becoming a dad, childhood milestones witnessed,
and the ways you and your offspring are alike.
By sharing these stories, you'll be lend-
ing your voice to their own chorus
of memories to create a
harmony that will
last a lifetime.

ALL ABOUT US

What was your child's or children's first word(s)? How did it feel when they spoke for the first time?

_____

_____

_____

_____

_____

_____

_____

_____

_____

Dreams are great. In fact, **DREAMS ARE NECESSARY IN LIFE** or no one would ever go anywhere! But a dream without a goal, and without action, has no opportunity to **COME TRUE**.

DENZEL WASHINGTON

From handcrafted art to store-bought souvenirs, what are your most cherished mementos of being a dad?

_____

_____

_____

_____

_____

_____

_____

_____

_____

_____

List all the cute nicknames (Nugget, Dumpling, or Buttercup, for example) you have used for your child/children. What are the names they have called you over the years?

_____

_____

_____

_____

_____

_____

_____

_____

Describe your favorite photograph of your child/children. Where are they, and what are they doing? Why is it so special to you?

_____

_____

_____

_____

_____

_____

_____

_____

What have been the funniest moments of fatherhood? Did your child say something at the worst possible time? Or maybe you've experienced an epic fail as a dad?

_____

_____

_____

_____

_____

_____

_____

_____

BECOMING A DAD

What was your reaction to learning you were going to be a dad for the first time? Describe the scene and your emotions.

_____

_____

_____

_____

_____

_____

_____

_____

_____

I understood once **I HELD A BABY IN MY ARMS** why some people have the need to keep having them.

SPALDING GRAY

Who was the first person you told you were going to become a father? How did you tell them, and how did they react?

_____

_____

_____

_____

_____

_____

_____

_____

_____

_____

What is one thing you wish someone had told you about being a dad before you welcomed your child into your life?

_____

_____

_____

_____

_____

_____

_____

_____

_____

Describe what it means to you to be a "good dad." Write about a specific moment when you felt like you had achieved this.

_____

_____

_____

_____

_____

_____

_____

_____

_____

_____

List three big fears you had about being a dad. Were they realized, or did it turn out to be not as scary as you thought?

_____

_____

_____

_____

_____

_____

_____

_____

MILESTONES IN FATHERHOOD

What milestone did your child or children reach that made you extremely proud and emotional?

_____

_____

_____

_____

_____

_____

_____

_____

"My daughters are yelling the lyrics to 'GIRLS JUST WANT TO HAVE FUN.' At that volume, it's not a song. IT'S A THREAT."

JAMES BREAKWELL

What milestones were you most excited for your child or children to achieve? For example—taking their first steps, hearing them say "I love you," or watching them graduate from high school or college? What about these experiences made them so memorable?

_____

_____

_____

_____

_____

_____

_____

_____

Describe the messiest experience you've had with your child or children.

_____

_____

_____

_____

_____

_____

_____

_____

_____

How and when did your child's/children's unique personality shine through for the first time? What was that experience like for you?

_____

_____

_____

_____

_____

_____

_____

_____

Describe the moment your child or children started to enjoy a TV show, listen to a certain kind of music, or found a new hobby that was different from your own interests.

_____

_____

_____

_____

_____

_____

_____

_____

SHARED TRAITS

When you first thought about being a dad, what three personality traits—like your sense of humor or empathetic nature, for example—did you hope to pass on to your children? Why?

_____

_____

_____

_____

_____

_____

_____

_____

_____

Children are smelly handfuls, but also **SWEET-SMELLING** sources of **ENDLESS SURPRISE AND JOY**. They are **HEARTACHE**, but also **HAPPINESS**. They are tears of sadness but also **TEARS OF JOY**. They come to have not only your physical traits but others as well.

FRED ZILIAN

Which unique quirks, like always having to say good night to everyone before bed, did you end up sharing with your offspring? In what ways are you and your child or children complete opposites?

_____

_____

_____

_____

_____

_____

_____

_____

What potentially unhealthy behaviors in your family history were you worried about being passed down? Did your child or children inherit any of them?

_____

_____

_____

_____

_____

_____

_____

_____

How do you and your child or children enjoy spending time together? For example, do you like making dinners, fishing, riding bikes, watching sports, or going to the movies together?

_____

_____

_____

_____

_____

_____

_____

_____

What talent does your child or children possess that you admire the most? How do you feel while observing them using it?

_____

_____

_____

_____

_____

_____

_____

_____

PART V

FATHERLY ADVICE

There may be periods of time when your child or children will not be open to receiving your advice. Over time, however, you hope they will come to recognize and appreciate that your life experiences can provide them with a wealth of knowledge. In the final part of the book, you will share important lessons learned, the dreams you still have for your child or children and the world at large, and how your legacy was and still is being shaped.

WATCHING THE WORLD CHANGE

Describe a famous moment in history you lived through. Where were you when it happened, and what was its lasting impact?

_____

_____

_____

_____

_____

_____

_____

_____

'There's **NO SHAME IN FEAR,**' my father told me, '**WHAT MATTERS IS HOW WE FACE IT.**'

GEORGE R.R. MARTIN

What has been the most meaningful invention during your lifetime?

_____

_____

_____

_____

_____

_____

_____

_____

_____

How do you see the world changing over the next 20 years?

_____

_____

_____

_____

_____

_____

_____

_____

_____

_____

What is something about the modern world—like social media, mobile banking, or talking to your home appliances—that your child or children would be surprised to learn that you enjoy?

_____

_____

_____

_____

_____

_____

_____

_____

Do you think dads today have it harder or easier than when you were a child, or is fatherhood simply different now? How so?

_____

_____

_____

_____

_____

_____

_____

_____

_____

LIFE LESSONS

What's the best piece of advice you have ever received about being a dad?

_____

_____

_____

_____

_____

_____

_____

_____

_____

"
If there is **NO STRUGGLE**, there is no **PROGRESS**.
"

FREDERICK DOUGLASS

Describe a time when your confidence was shaken. How did you respond, persist, and grow from that experience?

_____

_____

_____

_____

_____

_____

_____

_____

_____

_____

What's the one thing you wish you knew about life sooner? How would this knowledge have altered the course of your journey?

_____

_____

_____

_____

_____

_____

_____

_____

_____

List at least three secrets you've discovered to living a happy and healthy life.

_____

_____

_____

_____

_____

_____

_____

_____

_____

Describe a life lesson you imparted to your child or children by showing rather than telling. Was this an effective way of teaching?

_____

_____

_____

_____

_____

_____

_____

_____

_____

YOUR LEGACY

What is your code in life? What do you stand for and believe in?

_____

_____

_____

_____

_____

_____

_____

_____

_____

_____

I remember a **VERY IMPORTANT LESSON** that my father gave me when I was twelve or thirteen. He said, 'You know, today I welded a perfect seam, and **I SIGNED MY NAME TO IT**.' And I said, 'But Daddy, no one's going to see it!' And he said, 'Yeah, but **I KNOW IT'S THERE**.'

TONI MORRISON

If you could live your life all over again, which three things would you do differently? What would you not change?

_____

_____

_____

_____

_____

_____

_____

_____

_____

Describe your five most prized material possessions—for example, a classic car, the first edition of a book, or a favorite T-shirt. Why are they special to you?

_____

_____

_____

_____

_____

_____

_____

_____

_____

What has consistently motivated you to get out of bed each morning (aside from coffee or needing to use the bathroom)?

_____

_____

_____

_____

_____

_____

_____

_____

_____

_____

What is something you know how to do well? This could be speaking a foreign language, properly cooking a steak, or being respectful to elders. Have you passed this on to others?

_____

_____

_____

_____

_____

_____

_____

_____

HOPES AND DREAMS

If you were granted the power to make one change in the world that would immediately impact the entire planet, what would it be and why?

_____

_____

_____

_____

_____

_____

_____

_____

My dad always taught me to **NEVER BE SATISFIED**, to **WANT MORE**, and know that what is **DONE IS DONE**.

THIERRY HENRY

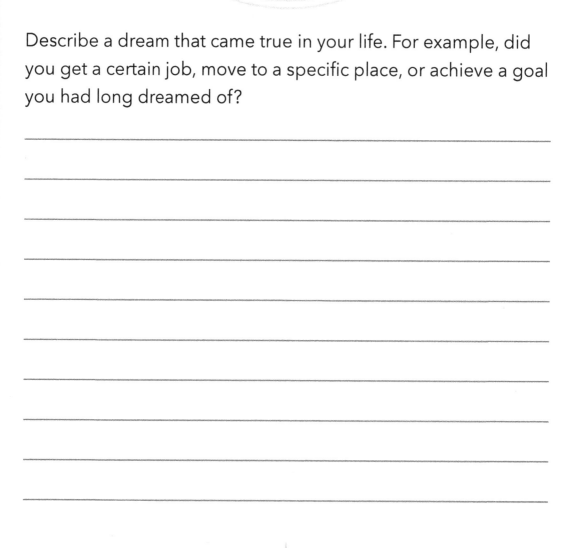

Describe a dream that came true in your life. For example, did you get a certain job, move to a specific place, or achieve a goal you had long dreamed of?

_____

_____

_____

_____

_____

_____

_____

_____

If money were no object, what place—be it a city, an island, or national park, for example—would be your dream to visit? Who would you take with you, and what would you want to do there?

_____

_____

_____

_____

_____

_____

_____

_____

In a dream world, where a movie is made from your life story, what's the title, and which actor would you want to play you?

_____

_____

_____

_____

_____

_____

_____

_____

_____

What do you have left to achieve, accomplish, and do? How will you go about making it happen? If you won't or can't reach for that dream, why?

_____

_____

_____

_____

_____

_____

_____

_____

ACKNOWLEDGMENTS

This book is dedicated to my dad, Donald J. Bogle, who supported my endeavors even when he didn't fully understand them and believed in me even when I did not (and too often, I didn't). He would always say that I was his good-luck charm, but really, I was the lucky one. I miss you every single day, Dad. I'm sorry I didn't ask more questions or help you document your story for Mom, your three children, seven grandchildren, and beyond. This book is also dedicated to you, the reader, and your family. Here's to never, ever letting our life stories go untold!

ABOUT THE AUTHOR

JEFF BOGLE is a son, brother, uncle, husband, friend, and (most proudly) the dad of two remarkable teenage daughters. He's also an Iris Award–winning photographer, avid traveler, storyteller, English football fanatic, and music lover. He has written about parenting, travel, family life, food, culture, and more for *The Washington Post*, *Fodor's*, *Parents Magazine*, *Good Housekeeping*, *Reader's Digest*, and *Esquire*, among other fine publications. This is his first book. Find him on Instagram and Twitter @OWTK. Jeff is also the publisher and editor-in-chief of *Stanchion*, a quarterly print literary and photography magazine. Learn more and subscribe at StanchionZine.com. He lives on a beautiful tree-lined street in the East Village neighborhood of New York City with his wife, one remarkable rescue pit bull, and four cats.

CPSIA information can be obtained
at www.ICGtesting.com
Printed in the USA
JSHW011710220122
22165JS00001B/1

9 781638 079569